THE INSANEL
GUIDE TO THE 2021 APPLE TV 4K

GETTING STARTED WITH THE LATEST GENERATION OF APPLE TV AND TVOS 14.5

SCOTT LA COUNTE

RIDICULOUSLY
SIMPLE BOOKS

ANAHEIM, CALIFORNIA

www.RidiculouslySimpleBooks.com

Table of Contents

Disclaimer: *Please note, while every effort has been made to ensure accuracy, this book is not endorsed by Apple, Inc. and should be considered unofficial.*

INTRODUCTION

Can you really cut the cable cord? Many people have, and Apple TV is one of the best solutions if you are ready to make the switch—or if you just want to have all of your channels and media in one place.

With stunning 4K support and the powerful A12 chip, the Apple TV can not only play movies and TV shows, but games!

This book will walk you through what you need to know—including how to use the new Siri Remote, and calibrate your TV with your iPhone for the best picture possible.

In covers:

- Apple TV interface
- Siri
- Apple Arcade
- Watching movies and TV shows
- Using the remote
- And more!

[1]

WELCOME TO STREAMING

This chapter will cover:
- What's Apple TV?
- What's the difference between models?
- What's in (and not in) the box?
- Using remotes and gestures
- Setting things up

YOUR MOVIES AND TV...ON DEMAND

Some people have said Apple's playing catch-up in the control for the living room. That's definitely not the case. The Apple TV we know today has been around since 2007 (albeit in a much different form), but Apple has been innovating in the living room for years. The Macintosh Television and Apple Interactive Television Box both tried to make it into the consumers living room in the nineties. And both failed. People just weren't ready—not to mention they were expensive ($2,000+).

The first official Apple TV was a bit beefier than what you see on selves today; it also had a hard drive because you had to actually download the content. The problem from the start was two-fold: one, it was more complicated than most consumers wanted; two, it didn't really do anything.

There was actually a third problem: cable television. Cable companies were doing everything possible to make sure cable channels like ESPN and HBO stayed exactly where they had existed for years—and they had the muscle to make sure it happened. As more consumers began adopting both media devices like Apple TV and Roku, and more "channels" like Netflix began popping up to provide cheap streaming content, cable channels took note: if they didn't adopt new strategies, they would not survive.

Currently Apple TV offers dozens of channels (some free, some not), but from the start, Apple has made it clear what they wanted: streaming that makes sense. Instead of paying for bundled cable to get all these channels you don't even want, Apple wants to begin offering a pay-as-you-go and individual option. That means you might one day pay only for the channels that you want. As Disney,

Time Warner, NBC, CBS, and more enter the streaming wars, this is certainly becoming more of a reality.

This strategy was first laid out with HBO Now, but Apple was very clear that this is just a preview of what's to come.

While other companies like Amazon Fire TV and Google Chromecast, tout more channels, the channels often are full of content you'd never watch. Apple is focused on quality content. Apple, at least for now, is often the first company that content providers come to. That means if you want channels like ESPN, then it's most likely going to come to Apple TV...and everyone else a few months later.

With the newest Apple TV, you'll experience something similar to what you have come to expect on the iPhone and iPad. Most notably, you'll be able to download apps (remember, apps are currently only on the new Apple TV—not the cheaper model; this is because apps require a hard drive, and the drive on the older model simply is not large enough).

What's the Difference Between All the Models?

Apple has kept a pretty similar look to the Apple TV for several years. The small black squarest design is simple, but it works. That's great! So why upgrade? What's the different between the latest generation and the previous generation? Both are 4K, so why upgrade?

Let's take a closer look. To start with, let's look really quick at how they're the same.

Both generations are the same design, weight and dimensions. Both support 2160p, 1080p, 720p, 576p, and 480p over an HDMI cable. Both support Dolby Atmos. Both have a gigabit ethernet input. Both support Bluetooth 5 and AirPlay 2. And, finally, both with either 32GB or 64GB of storage.

Okay, so how are they different? To start with, the most obvious difference is speed. The first generation uses a 2.38 A10X chip; the second generation uses a 2.49 A12 Bionic chip—what does that mean? It's fast. It's great if you love Apple Arcade—and don't forget you can pair Bluetooth game controller with it!

Next, the first generation supports WiFi 5; the second supports WiFi 6. That won't matter for most people, but as wireless bands improve, this is going to give you a stronger and faster wireless connection.

The newest standard of HDMI (2.1) is supported on generation 2 (HDMI 2.0a is on the first generation); again, this isn't a big difference, but it is important on newer TVs, as it will give truer color. The second generation Apple TV also supports high framerate HDR (up to 60-fps). If you have an iPhone 12 Pro (which shoots videos in this framerate), you'll be able to AirPlay it and show the best quality.

Finally, there's the new Siri remote. This is both a downgrade and upgrade. It's a downgrade in the sense that it doesn't include an accelerometer or gyroscope—that means you can't use it to play games like the old remote; but if you like playing games on Apple TV, then connecting a controller was always the best solution. The new remote, however, is also and upgrade in the sense that it got rid of a feature many people didn't like: the touchpad. It also added a mute button.

Here's the good news if you have the first-generation Apple TV and don't want to upgrade, but you hate the remote: you can buy the remote without the Apple TV. It's $59.

The biggest reason to upgrade is it futureproofs your Apple TV for years to come. If you have the first generation, there's not a big reason to upgrade—especially sense you can just buy a new remote. But if you've never owned an Apple TV, then get ready for a fast media box with arguably the best TV UI out there.

What's in the Box, What's Missing

The newest Apple TV is available at most online retailers and a growing number of big box stores; it's not uncommon for stores to run big discounts; it comes in two sizes—32GB ($149) and 64GB ($199). What's in the box of this device? The same as the previous generation. The remote, however, has been revamped (more on how to use it later in the chapter).

Notably absent is an HDMI cable. Some stores will try and highlight this fact and tell you about the fanciest HDMI cable money will buy; they'll try and sell you on the fact that it being gold will actually make everything superior. These so-called superior cables will cost anywhere from $20 to $50.

If you want the best deal on an HDMI cable, then go online where they cost about ten bucks; it doesn't have the fancy packaging that shows how awesome it is, but I bet you won't notice any difference once you plug it in.

The device is also missing an Ethernet cable. This is an optional add-on. Because the Apple TV streams content (vs. downloading it) then you'll obviously need Internet. Most people have Wi-Fi in their house, but some don't. If you're one of the houses that don't, then a cheap Ethernet cable would plug into the back of the Apple TV, and go directly into one of the ports on back of your Internet Router; you should have an empty port, but on the rare chance that you don't, you can buy an adaptor for a few bucks. I have Wi-Fi, but have my Apple TV plugged into the Internet because it gives the most stable connection.

How do you know if you have Wi-Fi? Your phone company will tell you, but a good indicator would be how you use the Internet. Do you have a laptop? Does the laptop have to plug into anything for Internet? If not, then it's probably connecting to a wireless connection. You'll need to know the password to it when you set up the Apple TV.

Unlike previous Apple TVs, there is no output for an optical cable.

Previous generation Apple TVs also had a USB-C port; this was for developers and really had no advantage to consumers, and it has been removed.

THE APPLE TV HARDWARE

So that's what's not in the box, but what's in the box? The hardware inside the device, that is.

Apple loves simple. That's pretty clear when you look at the box. There's not even a power button! Hitting the menu on the remote powers it on, but how do you power it off if there's no button?! Simple: you don't! The box will time out and turn itself off when not in use. You'll know it's on when you see a tiny LED light turn on in the front of the device. You can do this manually, and I'll show you how in the book.

The back, however, has a few different things to note:

In the diagram above, you'll find the power receptacle on the left. This is where you'll plug in the lone cable that came in your Apple TV box. Next to that, you'll find the HDMI slot on top (where you'll connect your television to the device), and a USB-C port above that. Remember, the USB-C isn't on the newest 4K Apple TV—that's one of the easiest ways to tell if you have the 4K Apple TV.

USING THE REMOTE

The remote control is also ridiculously simple! If you have the original remote, below is a guide on how to use it. I'm including this here (even though this is not the remote that comes with your device) because it's compatible with your device—it's a cheaper option if you lose your remote or want a backup one. Just an up/down, left/right controller and three buttons. It's not your grandma's remote, that's for sure!

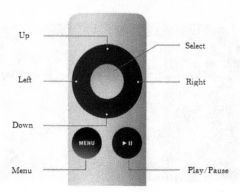

Here's a rundown of what each button does:

- Up/Down/Left/Right – These are the 'navigation' buttons, used to move around the various menus and items on the screen. Left and Right are also used for rewinding and fast-forwarding, which we'll discuss a little later.
- Select – This button, located in the center of the navigation buttons, is used to select items on-screen.
- Menu – This button is used to return to the main menu, or move up one menu when you're in a sub-menu. Think of it as the universal 'back' button.
- Play/Pause – As the name suggests, this button will begin or pause playback of your content, whether it's a video, music, podcast—it's universal.

As with pretty much any Apple product, things are not always as they appear on the surface. As we get into more advanced topics, you'll see how holding a button longer will do more things. Here are two examples:

- Hold Select for Six Seconds – This will put your Apple TV into 'Standby Mode'. If you don't, then it will eventually power itself down after several minutes. Standby means it's not fully off; unless you unplug it, the Apple TV will always be on, but it won't really be consuming much power, so don't worry!
- Hold Menu and Down for Six Seconds – It's rare, but the Apple TV "might" freeze or become unresponsive. If this ever were to happen, then this would reboot the device. It's kind of like CTRL, ALT, DELETE on a Windows computer. But chances are you'll never have to do this.

The 4th and 5th Apple TV remote completely reimagines the previous one, but don't worry—it's still easy to use and most the buttons are actually the same.

SIRI REMOTE (FIRST GENERATION) VS. SIRI REMOTE (SECOND GENERATION)

As mentioned previously, the new generation Siri remote can be purchased separately for $59. Alternatively, you can use the remote that came with your TV—just use the Learn Remote option under settings.

Side by side, the two remotes are about the same size. The new remote is slightly taller.

In thickness, however, the new remote is noticeably thinker. It's also encased in a stronger material that feels like a MacBook.

The new remote also features a Siri button on the side, which makes it much easier to find in a dark room.

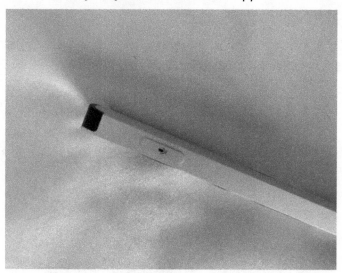

GENERATION 2 SIRI REMOTE

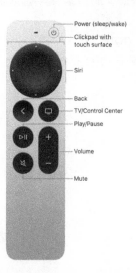

While the new remote doesn't have a touch pad that looks like the old remote, the round circle is a touch surface, so it's used in a similar way. Below the round circle is the Back button (called menu on the old remote and TV button, which gets you back to the home screen.

Below is the play / pause, mute and volume. The mute button is new on the generation 2 Siri remote.

At the very top of the remote is a power button; press it twice to turn the TV off (on the old remote, you would double press the menu button). Finally, on the side is the Siri button.

GENERATION 1 SIRI REMOTE

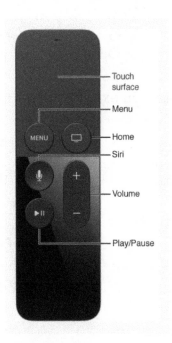

Here is a rundown of what the buttons do:

- Touch Surface – Obviously, the biggest enhancement to the remote is a built-in touch pad. When the keyboard appears, you'll use this to swipe around to the letters you want—pressing it down to use that letter. The same is true when navigating menus.
- Menu – Think of Menu like a back button; pressing it will go back one menu screen.
- Home – Where menu takes you back one screen, Home takes you back several (back to the main menu screen).
- Siri – Pressing and holding the mic button will bring up the Apple TV's Siri option; you can say things like Play (say movie name) or Open (say app name).
- Play / Pause – Play and Pause do exactly what you expect: play or pause the movie.
- Volume – Volume turns your TV volume up or down.

PAIR YOUR SIRI REMOTE

Pairing a new remote is simple. Press a button, then put it next to the Apple TV. That's it! No going to settings—just hold it close and your done in seconds.

> ### Pairing Remote
> Bring it closer to your
> Apple TV to continue pairing.

REMOTE SHORTCUTS

Below are a few remote shortcuts not so obvious.

Touch Surface

If you want to rearrange apps on your main Home screen, hover over an app, then press and hold the Touch Surface until it starts to jiggle; next swipe to where you want to move it.

On the keyboard, you can press and hold the Touch Surface over a letter to bring up an expanded menu of options (such as Uppercase and Accents).

Menu Button

Press the Menu button twice from the Home screen to start the screensaver.

Press and hold the Menu and Home buttons together to restart the Apple TV.

Home Button

Press the Home button twice to bring up the App Switcher, which displays all apps open. Swipe up on Touch Surface to force close an app.

Press the Home button three times quickly to access VoiceOver, which will dictate what you are seeing on the screen.

Press and hold the Home button to place the Apple TV in Sleep mode or to restart it.

Siri Button

Press the Siri button once and wait to view a list of commands you can ask Siri.

Play / Pause Button

Press the Play / Pause button once to change the keyboard between uppercase and lowercase.

Press the Play / Pause button once to delete an app in wiggle mode, which requires hovering over an app and holding down the touch surface until the icon starts to jiggle.

THERE'S AN APP!

The Apple TV remote is arguably the best streaming remote out there. But if you are like me, then you can never find it! What's great about Apple TV is it works perfectly with other iOS devices; if you have an iPhone or iPad you can download the free Apple Remote app from the App Store.

Once you have it, you can access it from either your control panel...

Or by opening the app from your phone.

One very important thing to remember: you have to be on the same network! If you are using your phone's data but your Apple TV is connected to the Wi-Fi, it will say the Apple TV is unavailable.

The remote app looks and works just like the physical remote with one important difference. See the top of the remote that has a name? In the example below it says Living Room (3).

If you tap that, it will show all available Apple TVs in your house and let you toggle between them. This is useful if you have more than one Apple TV.

AIRPLAY

Apple works very well with Apple products. If you have an iPhone, iPad, or Mac you can show your screen on the TV with zero wires! It's all wireless. It's called Airplay. The catch here is you have to be on the same network. If your Mac, for example, is using a different wireless network for Internet than your Apple TV, then it won't work.

On an iMac or MacBook, you can Airplay by clicking on the Airplay button in the upper right corner of the screen. Just select the TV you want to show your screen on.

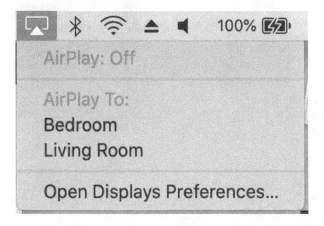

On an iPhone or iPad, just swipe down from the upper right corner to bring up your control panel, then tap on the Screen Mirroring button.

This will bring up all the available devices you can share your screen with.

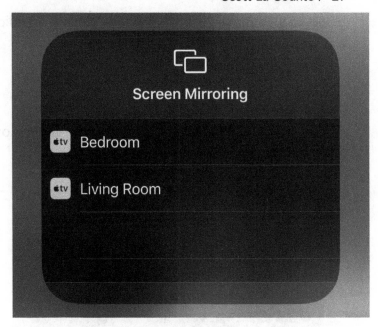

SETUP

So you know what Apple TV is; you know what's inside it. Now how do you use it? It's pretty simple to get started, but let me walk you through it.

First things first, however—get everything plugged in! Make sure the HDMI cable is connected and you've figured out if you have wireless or LAN Internet.

Once that's on, turn your TV on and to the input that the HDMI is connected to. Now hit the menu button on the remote. The first thing you'll see is a very easy to use setup screen.

At this point, you should also hear a robotic voice (Siri, for those of you with other Apple devices) explaining what's on your screen. This is a good way to make sure both your video and audio are working.

Setup is all guided by what you are seeing on the screen, so there's no need to repeat it here.

Once you are done, you'll be welcomed to a screen similar to the one below (with different movies showing most likely).

I know what your thinking—finally, time to get my movie on! But not so fast. First, it's a good idea to update the device to make sure you have the latest software installed. Will it work without it? Sure. But some of the things mentioned in this guide might not be there.

If you want to just follow along, that's fine, but take note of it because you'll probably want to update the device every month or so.

To begin the software update process, use your Apple remote to navigate to the 'Settings' icon, which is located all the way to the right on the top row of icons. Once there go to System > Software Updates and select Check for Update. If an update is available, a message appears. Select "Download and Install" to start downloading. During the update process make sure you don't disconnect your Apple TV. I'd recommend doing automatic updates, so you don't have to constantly see if they're available and your device is always up-to-date. If you'd like to do that, then go to settings, then System > Software Updates and select Update Automatically.

Update aren't always the quickest process, so don't start if you really want to watch a movie now! Most updates take about ten to thirty minutes. If you don't see the option to update or it's greyed out, then you have the latest version installed and there's nothing you need to do.

Once your update has been downloaded, your Apple TV will automatically begin the update process. This is a two-step process, requiring you to leave your Apple TV alone while it does its thing.

After a few moments, your Apple TV will automatically reboot and apply the update.

Once the process has completed, your Apple TV will boot into the Home screen, which will often feature a couple of extra icons and some things you can't see, like performance improvements. For the most part, it will look exactly the same with the exception of a new app icon. Changes are often under the hood.

[2]

THE APPLE TV INTERFACE

This chapter will cover:
- Overview of the User Interface
- Where / what things are
- Arranging apps

So now that you understand the controls, and you have the device updated to the most updated software, you are at last ready to use the device.

Let's jump back to the main menu, and get a little bit more familiar with it (remember, hitting the Home button gets you back to the main menu / Home screen.

There are two main parts to the Home screen: the header and the icons:

As you can see from the screenshot above, the header is the section Apple uses to promote the latest content (in the above example, that's a shot of the Apple TV show See—I was hovering over the Apple TV icon). It's here where you'll see new shows and movies available for purchase.

The header also changes depending on what icon you are on. If you move it over to TV, it will be the latest TV shows; music will be the latest music.

If you want to find out more about any of the advertised content, just hover over it and press down on the touch pad. The same is true of the icons. Pressing select on TV, movies or music will open a store dedicated to that icon.

The best way to think about these "icons" is as applications…or apps—kind of like the apps on your phone. As of this writing, Apple TV has 100s of so-called apps; some are from companies you know, but many are from upstart companies and hobbyist developers.

The first set of icons, which make up the two rows, are the ones you'll be using most often—at least until you download your favorite apps and start to move the icons around. They are:

- Apple TV – I know what you are thinking: this is where you go to see those Apple TV shows you are hearing about, right? You aren't wrong. But Apple TV is more than that. It's actually where you go to find out what to watch next. The AI inside the Apple TV starts taking note of what you do on Apple TV as soon as you watch it. I watch the Mandalorian on TV+; I don't have to set an alarm for when the next episode airs; as soon as it comes on, it's added to the Up Next area of Apple TV. It's as if the TV knows exactly what I'll watch next!

- Movies – This is where you'll go to rent and watch movies; if you own digital copies of movies (you can get those by redeeming vouchers that come in many Blu-rays) this is where those would be as well. If you have DVDs and Blu-rays that you want digital copies of, you can take them to Walmart or Vudu.com and redeem them for digital copies for a price; these digital copies, however, will not show up here; they will show up in the Vudu app; you need to connect Vudu to another app called Movies Anywhere; once you do, they'll be in your movie library with all of your other movies.
- TV Shows – This is where all the latest TV shows will be available to rent or purchase; from here you can also buy a season pass to a TV show—which means you pay for every show in advance and they become available to watch as the show airs. Usually you can get a discounted price by purchasing shows this way.

- Music – This is where you'll go to play music you've already purchased through iTunes.
- Computers – This is where you'll find content stored on your 'Home Sharing' enabled computers. Home sharing will be talked about in greater detail later, but for now, just know that this is how you can connect devices to the Apple TV.
- Settings – This is where all of the changeable settings for your Apple TV are located.

Once you're within any of these applications, pressing the menu button will take you one step back. Pressing the Home button on the remote will bring you back to the Home screen.

APP FOLDERS

In chapter 5, I'll cover how to move apps and create folders. Until then, just understand that like your phone or tablet, you'll probably start getting a lot of apps, which will make it more difficult to find what you want. Folders can be made to help your Apple TV stay organized.

[3]

WATCHING MOVIES AND TV SHOWS

This chapter will cover:
- Watching movies and TV shows
- Finding movies and TV shows
- Buying movies and TV shows

THE BASICS

So we've looked at how to get your account set up. Now let's learn how to spend money! This section will walk you through the Movies / TV shows portion of the device.

First, let's discuss movies. A couple quick things to note:

- The Apple TV has thousands of movies and prices change regularly.
- Most (but not all) of them are available for purchase, at a price anywhere from a few dollars up to about $19.99 (with bundles going slightly higher).
- Each week, Apple offers great discounts. Newer movies are often $9.99. Older movies often also drop in price if they have a sequel coming out. Lately, Apple has been offering movies for $3.99 to $4.99 on the weekends—usually they feature one or two of these. But these discounts are always changing, so that $4.99 may not be forever. A website I like to regularly visit is www.Bluray.com; this website has a section for iTunes and it lets you sort by lowest price.
- Most movies are available for rental, but not all; frequently a movie is released a few weeks before the physical copy is available, and they can be purchased but not rented until the street date. Some movies are also available to rent when they are in movie theaters. These movies cost more—sometimes up to $12.99. You pay a premium for not going to the theater.

- These rentals can be purchased at any time, and your viewing window (which is 24 hours in the US) only begins when you begin playing it. They can also only be watched on the device it's purchased; so if you rent it on your phone, it won't show on the Apple TV. Or if you rent it on the TV in the bedroom, you can't watch it on the one in the living room.
- After the 24 hours (if you've started it) or 30 days (if you haven't), the movie will disappear from your library.

Now that we've got the basic details out of the way, let's get started with movies by highlighting the Movies or TV icon and pressing select. Two things to note here: one, I'm saying Movies or TV—that's because while these are two separate sections, they work almost identically; two, you can also do this through the Apple TV icon, and I'll cover the difference later in the book.

Once you've pressed over the icon, you'll be presented with the iTunes store, separated into three parts. The top, which is a horizontal menu:

And the rest of the application, which follows the Home screen header-content pattern.

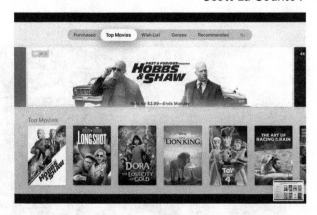

Moving around the screen using the directional buttons will highlight any of the content on display. Go ahead and highlight a movie from any of the rows below the header and press select. That will open up the movie or show.

If it's a TV show, then you'll see options to purchase different episodes or seasons. Movies are a bit more minimal: you can buy it (or, depending on the movie, rent it), preview it, or add it to your wish list.

Get an extended description.

Add to your iTunes Wish List.

Select to buy.

Watch a preview.

The 'More' menu item might escape your notice—you have to pan down with your remote. Don't let it. It's a fantastic compendium of reviews (both professional and user created), as well as a portal to other movies you might be interested in.

As you can see, there is a critics' review section (courtesy of Rotten Tomatoes), followed by customer reviews, and then a detailed list of the people responsible for the film. Highlighting and selecting any of those names will bring up a list of other available titles featuring that person.

Navigating with your remote, you can now head to any of these other movies to bring up that movie's page, which will function in exactly the same way as The Maze Runner did in our example. This won't be all the movies the actor has done— just the ones on iTunes. It's also worth noting that you should turn on parental settings—unless you don't mind little ones seeing R-Rated movies, because even if it's a kid's movie, recommendations for adult movies might still come up.

To get back to the movie's page, press the menu button on your remote.

Once you've purchased something, you'll be presented with a confirmation screen. Tap 'OK' to confirm. You don't have to wait for it to download—you can watch it almost immediately—it may take a few seconds depending on the speed of your Internet.

Normally, playing a movie is really quick. Every now and then it will say a ridiculously long amount of time (I've seen it as high as 16 hours until it can play); usually it's a glitch or a bad Internet connection. You can try two things. One, check your Internet connection (I use SpeedTest.net from my computer to see the speed); if it's slow, then either wait or restart your Internet; the second reason is it's just a glitch (which is rare); restarting your Apple TV will usually fix it. The last thing you can try is to simply wait. Usually if it says a long wait like 16 hours, it will change pretty quickly. But, like I said, waiting more than a few seconds for a movie to load is pretty rare.

If you choose to watch something later, you'll find it in the horizontal menu under 'Purchased.' Purchases can be found under either 'Recent Purchases' or under the genre of the show or movie; you can also find it by searching for it. I have over

200 shows in my library—I must spend a lot of money on TV shows, right? Not exactly! In the TV store, there's a section called Free Shows; I get a lot of shows there—these are full length episodes usually released before a show comes out (often they're pilot episodes). I've also found a number of documentaries there.

If you have some idea of what you'd like to watch, the horizontal menu also includes an item labeled 'Search.' Pressing select here will bring up a search window, where you can search by title, actor, director, or even subject.

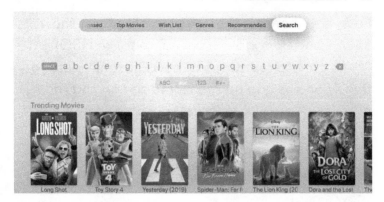

Instead of searching, however, do what the new Apple TV was built for and does well: use Siri; for Siri commands, see the next section of this book.

Not sure what to watch? You can see recommendations based on what you have previously watched.

Buying TV shows is the same as movies...sort of. TV shows are generally available in two different ways:

As standalone episodes (usually for $1.99 to $2.99 each—HD versions are more than SD; just like movies). Or as entire season (called Season

Pass, anywhere from $15.99 for broadcast shows to $59.99 and up for premium content like HBO).

To get started with TV shows, just navigate to the TV Shows app on the Home screen and then press select. You'll be greeted with a screen that looks the same as the Movies app does. Browse around for something that interests you, and then press select. You'll be greeted with that television show's page.

MOVIE / TV PLAYBACK

If you are like me, you probably like special features on a movie; for most movies, you still get that. There's a section called "Extras" of "Features" when you go to a movie (right before you select play). TV shows don't have this, but at the end of the season (after all the episodes), you'll usually see featurettes from the show that are available if you bought the entire season.

Pushing play and pause seems easy enough; but let's talk briefly about playing a movie because there are a few controls you might have missed.

When you push play / pause, you'll see a bar that looks a bit like this:

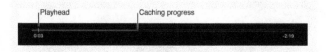

You are seeing two things: one, where you are in the movie (labeled the playhead); two, the caching—caching is something you see when streaming a movie, and it means how much of the movie has downloaded; if the Internet stops but you have cached 10 minutes of the movie, that means you have 10 minutes you can watch with no Internet. The cache is temporary and deletes itself with no effort from you. If it's cached, you can also jump ahead without waiting for it to download.

While the movie is paused, you can also swipe left or right and see a thumbnail preview of the movie scene, and then press the touch pad to play the movie starting at that preview.

If you want to quickly go back or forward just 10 seconds, you can do so by swiping your touch surface left or right (left for back and right for forward).

One of the new play back features is to get information about the movie / TV show while it's playing. To get this, swipe your touch surface downward. That brings up a screen like the one below.

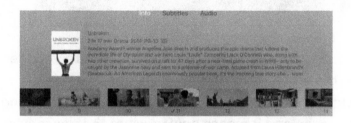

Along with information about what you are watching, you can also swipe over to add subtitles (if available) and change the spoken audio language (if available).

Under audio there are also a few other choices besides language. If you are watching a particularly loud movie but don't want all the loudness, for example, you can go to this section to reduce loud noises.

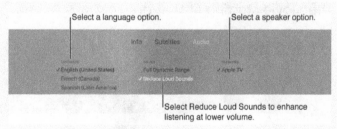

Select a language option.   Select a speaker option.

Select Reduce Loud Sounds to enhance listening at lower volume.

If you have an AirPlay speaker this is also where you would add it; the same is true with Bluetooth speakers / headsets that are set up to the device.

CONTROL CENTER

Apple has been on a mission for sometime to make all devices feel the same—so if you use an iPhone, you'll see familiarity when you use iPad, Apple TV or any other device.

One place you see this is the control center. Press and hold the Home button on your Siri remote.

If you have HomeKit Connect devices, you'll see them here, but you can also use this area to toggle between users.

SHARE AUDIO WITH TWO DEVICES

Playing back audio to a Bluetooth headset is nothing new with Apple TV. In TVOS 14 this gets even better with the ability to playback to multiple devices. This is great for parents who want to watch TV while their kids sleep!

To get started, press and hold the home icon (⬚) on your Siri remote. This brings up the control panel. From here, click the audio controls icon (⊚); this will show all available devices. Select all the devices you want to AirPlay to (it can be supported BlueTooth speakers as well)

PICTUREN IN PICTURE

One of the biggest improvements to TVOS 14 was the ability to watch two things at the same time with picture-in-picture mode.

Big as the feature is, you probably won't notice it, because it's a little hard to find at first. It also doesn't work on all apps—so if you follow these steps, but don't see what I'm talking about then there are probably two things happening: one, you haven't updated to TVOS 14 or great; two, the video you are trying to perform picture-in-picture with is not currently supported.

This mode also works well if you have a HomeKit enabled camera—for example, you can set it to show a picture-in-picture when someone is at the front door.

Turn Picture in Picture On / Off

To turn the mode on start playing a video as you normally would. Next, pause the video with your remote. While the video is paused, swipe up with the Siri remote.

Swipe up to the picture in picture icon:

If you don't see the icon, then it is not currently supported.

To close the picture in picture window tap the touch surface of the remote, and move to the picture in picture window. This icon will expand it to full size again:

And this icon will close the picture in picture window:

Controlling Picture in Picture

There are a few other icons you might see as you control picture in picture.

The following will close the window if you are finished with the video.

To move a picture in picture window to another area, use this icon:

[4]

SIRI

This chapter will cover:
 • How Siri works on Apple TV

I hate to be the bearer of bad news, but cable cutting isn't what it used to be. Cable cutting a few years ago meant you were somewhat of a rebel. You were sticking it to the man and saving lots of dollars every month in the process.

The thing is, however, businesses caught on to the idea of cable cutting pretty quickly. Everyone and their mother wanted to make money in the streaming wars.

Siri

If you bought the new Apple TV, you are paying a premium for two major features: apps and Siri integration. Siri can do a lot, but it's still a little limited. Here are a few of the standard commands available:

- What should I watch tonight?
- Find (say movie)
- Play (say episode number / season number) of (say TV name)
- Show (say genre [i.e. comedies, action, documentaries, etc.])
- Find (say actor / actress name) movies
- TV shows / movies for kids
- Show (say PG / PG-13 / etc.) movies
- Show (combine genres [such as romantic comedies or action / romance])

When you are playing a movie or TV show, here are a few things you can say:

- Pause this
- Play from the beginning
- Skip forward (say number of seconds / minutes)
- Go back (say number of seconds / minutes)
- Turn on / off closed captioning
- Turn on / off (say subtitles [Spanish, French, etc. {when available}])
- What did he / she say?

As noted, Siri is limited, but you can still ask general informative questions on the Home screen—such as the below:

- Who won the NBA Finals / Stanley Cup / Laker Game, etc.?
- Where is XYZ team playing tomorrow / tonight?
- Who is the starting pitcher for the dodgers?
- What's the weather?
- What's the weather in (say city)?
- When is sunset?
- When is sunset in (say city)?
- How is (say stock) today?

Siri is always expanding its database, so try it out—if something's not here, then ask it anyway.

[5]

MUSIC AND PODCAST

This chapter will cover:
- Streaming music
- Discovering music
- Podcasts

So now you know how to use the device and buy content. Now let's get the most out of it. The best part of this section is some of the best content is free.

First things first...let's talk about audio. I know you probably bought the Apple TV for movies and TV, but there's a lot of great stuff you can listen to.

I'm going to talk very briefly about Podcasts, which is where you'll find some of the best original content out there. But first, let's look at music.

MUSIC

Music, for a long time, was one of the few stores missing on Apple TV; you could listen to what you had already bought on iTunes, but you couldn't actually buy it from the TV itself. This changed about a few years ago.

If you want a lot of music, then I suggest checking out iTunes Match (see: http://www.apple.com/itunes/itunes-match/). You probably have a lot of MP3s on your computer—and if we're being honest, some of them were probably shared with you by a friend or obtained in a way that's a little...questionable. For $24.99 a year, Apple will go through your computer and everything that's music will be added to a music cloud—even if you never actually bought it. Once it's in the Cloud, you can stream it from your Apple TV or any other Apple device.

Personally, I think the best deal, however, is Apple's music subscription: Apple Music. Plans start at just $9.99 (even cheaper if you are a student) and this gives you access to Apple's library of thousands of songs and artists.

The Music app on Apple TV is very similar to iOS (and don't forget, if you buy it for your phone, you also get it on all of your other devices—including Apple TV).

When you open the app, you'll have a menu bar across the top with all the different places that you can go in the app.

For You is recommendations based on what you have been listening to.

Not digging those recommendations? You can also browse genres in the Browse menu. In addition to different genre categories, you can see what music is new and what music is popular.

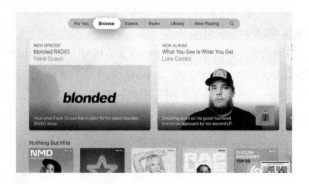

Videos are music videos for hit songs.

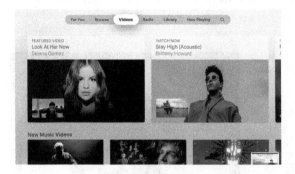

Radio is Apple's version of AM / FM; the main radio station is Beats One. There are on-air DJs and everything you'd expect from a radio station.

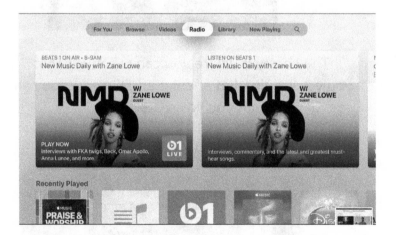

While Beats One is Apple's flagship station, it's not its only station. You can scroll down and tap on Radio Stations under More to explore and see several other stations based on music styles (i.e. country, alternative, rock, etc.). Under this menu, you'll also find a handful of talk stations covering news and sports. Don't expect to find the opinionated talk radio you may listen to on regular radio—it's pretty controversy-free.

The library is where you can see music that you've downloaded or own; additionally, you can see playlists that you've created.

Now Playing is pretty basic. It shows what's currently playing (if anything); if nothing is playing, then it is blank.

The last option is the search menu, which is pretty self-explanatory. Type in what you want to find (i.e. artist, album, genre, etc.).

PODCASTS

You've probably heard all about Podcasts, but if you haven't actually listened to one, then you are really missing out!

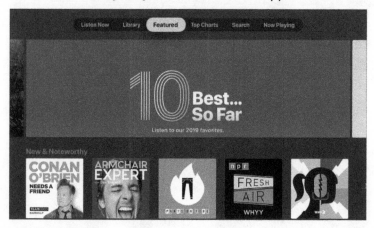

Podcasts can be anything from news programs to comedy shows, and everything in between. Because anyone can start a Podcast, there are literally thousands to choose from. Some good...some not. But what's really cool about Podcasts is the sheer scope of topics covered—there's really something for everyone here. Entire shows are devoted to niches like Disney history or horrible movies.

Podcasts aren't like regular radio shows. They don't come on at a set time (though some do); some Podcasts are weekly, others are daily, and still others come on for a few weeks then drop away without any explanation.

The best part about Podcasts is they're free.

If you've never delved into the world of Podcasts, you're in for a treat. ITunes practically invented the market for Podcasts, and it shows. So let's take a look at how to get them to work on Apple TV.

To get started with Podcasts, head to the Podcast app on your Home screen and press select to open the Podcast Store. There's a lot to choose from.

Feel free to browse the store in the same way you have previously for TV shows and movies. It functions in the same way. You can also search for anything you want by using the search bar—so if you know a comedian has a Podcast, search for his name.

[6]

THERE'S AN APP FOR THAT TV

This chapter will cover:
- Finding, installing, and removing apps
- Apple Arcade
- iBooks for Apple TV
- Arranging apps

Aside from the Movies, TV Shows, and various music-related apps we've discussed so far, there are literally hundreds of other apps to try out. Some of them you'll find useful, while others you might never use.

The App Store takes a lot from the store you are familiar with on iPhone and iPad; actually, it looks surprisingly identical to that store. If you've never used an iPhone or iPad and don't know how to use the store, don't worry: it's very simple and I'll show you how.

Don't know what app you want? Apple regularly curates its own picks and puts them in the Discover section.

When you see an app that you want to find out more about, use your touch pad and press down. This will give you a description of the app along with a few screenshots.

If the app has an "Open" button, then you already have it (some developers have released their iPhone / iPad apps on Apple TV as well and they will allow you to download it free—which is why it might say you already own it when you never purchased it on the TV); if it says "Get" the app is free; if there's a cloud icon, it's an app you own and can re-download; and finally if there's a price then you would have to buy it.

Once it's done downloading, it will automatically appear on your Home screen and you'll need to delete it if you want it removed.

If you enable Family Members in iTunes, then all of your shared apps will also appear.

Apps are updated regularly. To save you the hassle of having to check back for updates, the Apple TV downloads updates automatically. If you want this feature turned off, then go to your Home screen, then Settings, Apps and turn off Automatically Update Apps. To update an app manually, you have to go to that app in the App Store and see if an update is available.

If you have the smaller Apple TV, space might fill up quickly; you can remove apps and see what's using space by going to your Home screen, then Settings, General and Manage Storage; a list of the apps appears and shows you how much space each is using. If you want to remove an app, highlight the trash icon and then press down on the touch pad.

GAMES

Games might not be the first thing you think about when you buy an Apple TV, but it's quickly becoming one of its more popular features. There's a lot of power inside the Apple TV and it can handle some pretty large and graphic-intensive games.

If the thought of playing a game with that little remote seems a little daunting, then you are not alone. Yes, you can use that remote, but a better option is connecting a Bluetooth controller—you can even use Play Station and Xbox controllers!

APPLE ARCADE

Apple Arcade is one of Apple's newest services; think of it like Netflix for games. It's $4.99/month (nothing extra for other members of your family— share it with up to five members).

The price gives you access to 100+ games. Unlike some streaming services where you have to play the games online, Apple Arcade lets you download the games to play them offline. You can play them on all your Apple compatible devices: iPhone, iPad, and Apple TV. When you stop playing on your phone, you can start playing where you left off on your TV or iPad.

There are no ads and you can use it with parental controls.

How to Sign Up

Apple Arcade isn't an app. It's a service. You only download what you want. You sign up by visiting the App Store and tapping on Arcade. This brings you to the main Arcade menu where all you have to do is tap Subscribe.

Once you subscribe, you'll see a welcome menu.

The Arcade menu is now replaced by games you can download. Tap "Get" for any game you want. $4.99 is for everything—not per app.

When you read about the game, be mindful of the app size; if you have data restrictions, make sure you download it over Wi-Fi.

The app looks like every other app on your phone. The only difference is the splash screen, which says "Arcade."

CANCELLING ARCADE SUBSCRIPTION

All subscriptions are cancelled the same way. Go to the App Store and tap your account. Next, tap Subscriptions.

This shows you all of your active subscriptions, including Apple Arcade.

Once you click on it, there is an option to cancel on the bottom.

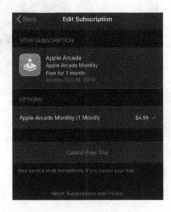

You will get a notification that all of your games will be erased after your subscription expiration (note: it expires on the original expiration date—not the date you cancel).

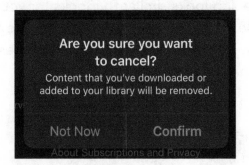

The subscription details now tell you when it's cancelled.

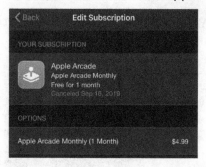

iBooks for Apple TV

One app that I'd recommend for parents is the iBooks app. Books for TV, you say? Yes! It's basically your young child's favorite book on the big screen—some are even interactive and have lively narrators. You can also, of course, read the book to your kid and use the remote to swipe to the next page.

The app looks similar to iBooks for your phone or table. There's a My Books tab that shows all of your books; just hover over them and press the touch pad to open.

And a Featured Books area to buy more books. Any picture book you have purchased on your other devices will show up in your library—only picture books. You can't read War and Peace on your big screen, unfortunately.

ARRANGING APPS, DELETING APPS, AND CREATING FOLDERS

Because you'll probably spend more time using apps like Netflix than apps like Sky News, it's helpful to have the apps arranged in a way where the most popular apps are near the top. To rearrange any of the apps, just hold down on the menu button over the app you want to move. After several seconds it will change appearance and you can move it around.

As you are doing this, you can press the play / pause button on your remote to bring up more options. From here, you'll be able to delete the app or create a new folder. Remember, if you delete an app, it's stored in the Cloud, so you can always reinstall it later.

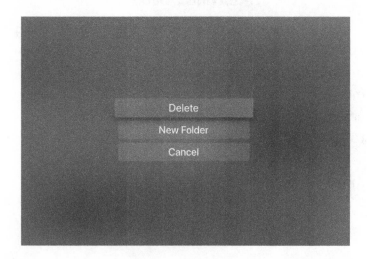

When you create a new folder, you'll be able to rename the folder to something that says what's inside the folder; anytime you want to add more apps to the folder, just follow the steps above to move the app, and drag it over the folder.

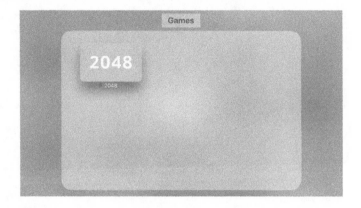

[7]
PHOTOS

This chapter will cover:
- Viewing photos on Apple TV

The Photos app on Apple TV is pretty straight-forward. Once you're signed into iCloud on the Apple TV, you will see the photos that are in your Apple TV library.

The top menu has four options. Photos is where you'll see all of your photos.

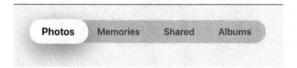

You probably have thousands of photos, so the next three sections make it easier to see the photo that you are looking for. These sections can only be viewed. You can't, for example, create an album on Apple TV—you make it on your phone, computer or tablet and then it shows up on Apple TV automatically.

Memories is always changing and showing things that happened during different months and years. When you click on them, you can play them like mini videos—it shows a slideshow with music and lasts a few seconds. It's an AI curated list—meaning you can't create memories to watch.

Shared is where you'll see photos that you've shared with other people.

Finally, Albums shows all the albums that are on your other iOS devices—some are created by you, but many will be automatically created. For example, there's an album just for videos and Live Photos.

[8]
APPLE TV

This chapter will cover:
- What is Apple TV
- How Apple TV works

I'll be honest: Apple TV is a little confusing—it's an app, it's the name of the device, and it's the name of the streaming services. So basically, you buy an Apple TV, but the Apple TV app is only sort of how you use it—and the Apple TV app doesn't just have Apple TV shows.

So, what exactly is Apple TV? Let's open the Apple TV app and look at it a bit closer.

The first thing you'll see when you open Apple TV—and the section you'll probably find yourself using the most—is Watch Now.

Watch Now is Apple's way of helping you find the content you want. Let's say you watch the TV show Superstore; you bought a season pass, so every week or so there will be a new episode. With Watch Now, that next episode will automatically go to your Up Next queue as soon as the episode hits the store, so you don't have to remember when it comes on or go and search for it.

The Up Next section will also add movies and TV you are still watching; so if you are binging a show on Netflix, but haven't finished it yet, you'll see it here.

Up on the top menu, you'll see options for movies, TV shows and more; those all work very similarly to their dedicated apps. Many of the sections, however, require you to buy content or download apps. For example, tap on Sports. This shows you live broadcasts of different events (content varies depending on what apps you subscribe to).

When you tap on the content, you'll see it gives you a message that asks you how you'd like to open it; when you tap that, it will give you options for different apps. You can also tap the Add to Up Next to add it to the Watch Now section, so it automatically updates when there's new content.

When you tap on library, it looks very similar to libraries in other sections of the Apple TV with one distinction: there's a section for 4K HDR. This shows you what apps you can stream in 4K (assuming you have the 4K Apple TV).

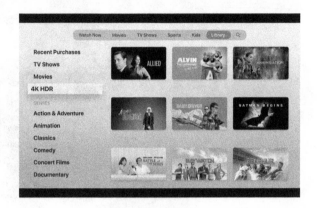

APPLE TV+

Apple has been quietly working on a TV service for quite some time. In 2019, they finally revealed the details. It is $4.99 a month (free for a year if you buy an iPhone, iPad, Apple Watch, Apple TV, or Mac—note that this may change in the future), and launched November 1.

To watch any of these shows, go to the TV app. It's available on Apple TV, iPad, and iPhone; it remembers your place, so if you pause it on one device, you can pick up where you left off on another.

As this is a different format, things could change at a later date, but as of the printing of this book, below is the current lineup of TV shows:

Dramas

- Amazing Stories (Science Fiction / Anthology)

- Defending Jacob (Crime Drama)
- For All Mankind (Science Fiction / Alternative History)
- Home Before Dark (Mystery)
- The Morning Show (Drama)
- See (Science Fiction)
- Servant (Thriller)
- Tehran (Thriller)
- Truth Be Told (Legal Drama)

Comedies

- Dickinson (Period Comedy)
- Ghostwriter (Family / Mystery)
- Little America (Anthology)
- Little Voices (Music / Comedy)
- Mythic Quest: Raven's Banquet (Workplace Comedy)
- Ted Lasso (Sports Comedy)
- Trying (Romantic Comedy)
- Central Park (Animated Comedy)

Kids

- Doug Unplugged
- Fraggle Rock: Rock On!
- Helpsters
- Helpsters Help You
- Snoopy In Space
- Stillwater

Featured Films

- The Banker (Drama)

- Greyhound (War)
- Hala (Drama)
- On the Rocks (Drama)

Docuseries
- Becoming You
- Dear...
- Earth At Night In Color
- Greatness Code
- Home
- Long Way Up
- Oprah's Book Club / The Oprah Conversation
- Tiny World
- Visible: Out On Television

Documentary
- Beastie Boys Story
- Boys State
- Dads
- The Elephant Queen

Shows and films are being added monthly, and current shows are getting future seasons, so look for this area to rapidly change.

[9]

SYSTEM SETTINGS

This chapter will cover:
- Overview of settings
- Restarting Apple TV

You probably are starting to see that Apple TV is really simple to use. Remember: Apple builds their devices in a way that's pretty disaster proof—that means you won't ruin anything by hitting the wrong button. So, take time to explore.

There are a few more things to cover; notably, the settings menu. Chances are you won't spend much time here, but you still want to know how to change a few things.

To get started with the settings menu, navigate to the System Settings app on the Home screen and press Select. Once you've done that, you'll be presented with the settings menu we briefly visited earlier.

As you can see, there are several different items within this menu. Some of these items also contain their own sub-menus (and even sub-sub-menus in some cases!). Let's take a moment to break them down, and then we'll discuss the most important things you'll find within them.

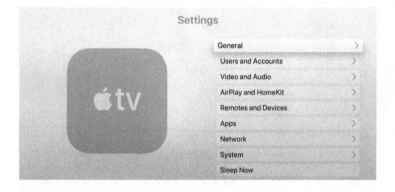

- General – This is where you'll find the vast majority of the changeable settings.
- Users and Accounts – Is where you can go to add or remove iCloud accounts.
- Audio and Video – This area contains settings for closed captions and languages, as well as various audio output options.
- Airplay – This section contains all of the options for Apple's 'Airplay' service, which we'll discuss a little later. You can turn the function off or on from here, and set a password for it if you like. You can also add Airplay devices—if, for instance,

you have a speaker that is Airplay compatible.

- Remotes and Devices – Where you can go to add a new remote or wireless video game controller.
- System – Where you can go to check for updates or do a factory reset (i.e. when everything is wiped off of your device.
- Sleep Now – Just in case it's not immediately obvious from this item's name, selecting this will put your Apple TV to sleep, which is the suspended animation state your Apple TV remains in when not in use. You can exit sleep by pressing any button on your remote.

GENERAL

Within the General tab there are only a couple of areas you might want to change.

The first is Screen Saver. This is where you can select what shows when your Apple TV is idle and how long before the Screen Saver activates.

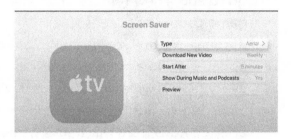

The next section you might want to update is restrictions. This lets you restrict certain apps and sections on TV; it also restricts who can buy content.

VIDEO AND AUDIO

You might want to use this menu if you don't want 4K videos. There's also an audio section you can use if you want audio to go to another device; for example, let's say you want video on your TV, but you want audio to play on your Homepod speaker. Go to Audio Output in this section to change that.

AIRPLAY AND HOMEKIT

Airplay and HomeKit have some options to change how a screen is displayed when you are Airplaying. Is it a Conference Room Display, for example?

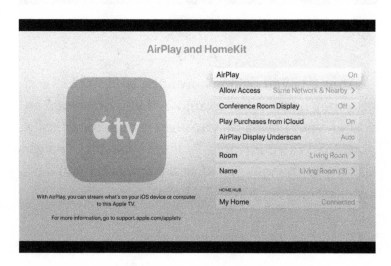

REMOTES AND DEVICES

This section lets you update what the buttons on the remotes do; you can also add third-party remotes and devices here (for example, a game controller.

APPS

Apps lets you decide how apps are installed and how they update. For example, if you download an app on your phone do you want it to automatically download to your Apple TV if it's available. You can also make changes to individual apps that you have installed on your Apple TV here.

CALIBRATE YOUR TV COLOR

One of the newest features of TVOS is a new color balance setting that calibrates the TV using your iPhone, so you know that you have the best color quality possible. To use it, go to your Settings, then Video and Audio.

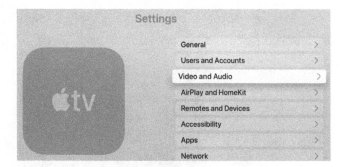

Next, go to Color Balance.

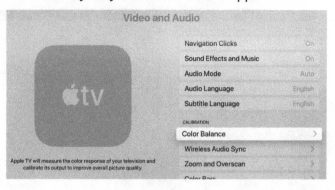

From here, you'll see a message about adjusting the color balance. You'll need your iPhone at this point.

As long as you are on the same WiFi network, you'll see a notification on your iPhone at this point. Swipe that.

A new message will swipe up on your iPhone. Tap "Continue."

The next message will show that everything is preparing and to hold your phone close to the screen.

Next, turn your phone so the front is facing the screen. Move it close to the screen and make sure it's within the border of the phone on the screen.

As you began the process, you'll see several colors flash on the screen.

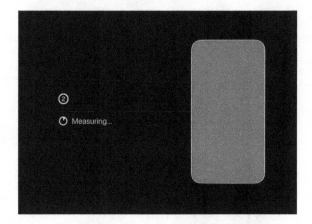

Continue to hold your phone to the screen until it tells you to remove it. Once you see "Color balance complete" you can remove your phone from the screen.

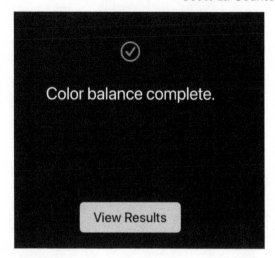

When you click "View Results" it will show you the optimization; click "Use Original" to see the old one; continue to toggle back and forth between the two screens.

SYSTEM

Finally, system lets you check for software updates, restart your device, and do a factory reset.

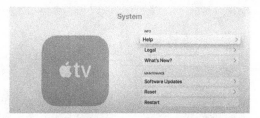

[10]

CABLE CUTTING

This chapter will cover:
- Truth about cable cutting
- Streaming services

Most of this book is about the Apple TV, but I want to leave you with one final section on cutting out cable—because, let's face it, if you have bought an Apple TV that's probably something you are very strongly considering.

Perhaps you are thinking, "Cable is expensive, but it is convenient." But is it really? Times have changed. Today, alternative methods are often more convenient.

Perhaps you are thinking, "Cable is simple. I don't want to learn another new technology." Most so-called "new technology" is easier to use than cable. A cable remote has over three dozen buttons—I bet you don't even know what all of them do. An Apple TV remote? It has two buttons on the old devices and three main buttons on the new one! What sounds easier to you? Learning dozens of buttons or learning two?

Unlike the rest of this book, this is not exclusively Apple. Most of the services referenced in this book can be used on other devices; you may have an Apple TV in your living room and a Roku in your bedroom; you subscribe to the service, not the app; most of the services let you stream to more than one device in your house.

This guide will show you all the alternatives as well as how to know what the best fit is for your lifestyle.

A RETURN TO BUNNY

When you think about antenna television, you probably think about standing in front of an old TV set moving bunny ears around trying to angle them just the right way for perfect reception. And by perfect reception, I mean there's static and fuzz, but you can make out what the person on the screen is saying.

Several years ago, over-the-air signals moved to digital signals; when picked up by the antenna, you will get picture quality that is just as sharp as cable. So for basic channels, you are paying the cable company a fee for something you can literally get for free.

What do you need to do this? If you still happen to have a non-HDTV, then you would need a converter box; that will cost you about $40; another $100 and you might as well get a new TV.

If you have an HDTV—these are the flat rectangular TVs—then you won't need any kind of converter box. You just need an antenna. It will cost you around $25; if you pop into RadioShack, Walmart, Target, Best Buy, or anywhere else with electronics, you can buy one for about that price—possibly a little cheaper. I've seen them as low as $10. If you live in a remote area or an area with a lot of signal interference, then a more expensive one will probably be a better fit.

Best of all, HDTV antennas are pretty slick and modern looking. They are normally square like the picture below. The days of bunny ears are pretty much gone.

This is definitely the cheapest way of cutting the cord, but what about recording TV shows? That's definitely a plus of cable. You can purchase a DVR for less than $200; unfortunately, this often requires a monthly plan, so if you are looking to cut the bill, and not add a new one, then this might not be the best option. There are DVRs that don't have a monthly fee.

So what are the cons? The biggest is what you are missing. If you only want local channels (ABC, CBS, NBC, etc.), then it's perfect. If you want ESPN, Disney, etc., then you will need to look further at alternatives.

THE TRUTH ABOUT CABLE CUTTING

I hate to be the bearer of bad news, but cable cutting isn't what it used to be. Cable Cutting a few years ago meant you were somewhat of a rebel. You were sticking it to the man and saving lots of dollars every month in the process.

The thing is, however, businesses caught on to the idea of cable cutting pretty quickly. Everyone and their mother wanted to make money in the streaming wars.

Do you know how much it would cost to subscribe to every streaming service out there? Over $350 a month! Yikes, right! And that doesn't even factor in the cost of having Internet to get those services.

STREAMING SERVICES

Of course, no one subscribes to all of them. Most people subscribe to two or three. In this section, I'll break down all the big services and how much they cost as of this writing. Keep in mind that many of these services are still in their infancy— that means they are cheap now, but are more than likely going to go up in cost as they get bigger. Almost all of these services have different tier costs, so I'm including the lowest price.

Word of advice: do your homework! Some of the new services have deals with other companies to give you the service for free. For example, I get

HBO Go with my cell phone service; it was a promo when I signed up. Some Verizon plans come with a year of Disney+.

Netflix (starting at $8.99 / month)

Netflix is, of course, the beast that started it all; they have thousands and thousands of movies and TV shows. They are spending billions on programing and some of the biggest talent in Hollywood is making original TV shows and movies with them. Some of the TV shows you'll find here: the science fiction series Stranger Things, the suspenseful Black Mirror, and dramatic The Crown. Their original movies have frequently caught the attention of big awards; these include: The Irishman, Roma, and The Ballad of Buster Scruggs.

Hulu (starting at $5.99 / month)

Hulu is a joint venture from a lot of companies (like Disney, Comcast, and NBC); this means you are going to find a lot of TV shows right after their original air date. Netflix has lots of shows, but you have to wait several months for them to come on; on Hulu, you have to wait about a day. If you want to cut the cord, but are worried about missing out on live TV, then check Hulu and see if your favorite shows are on it.

Amazon Prime Video (included with Prime membership; $8.99 / month without)

Amazon Prime Video is a no brainer if you have

Amazon Prime. It has a growing amount of original content (including Jack Ryan, The Man in the High Castle, and Bosch). You may notice that those TV shows are based on books (or book characters); Amazon licenses a lot of book content—they are currently working on a series based on J.R.R. Tolkien's Middlearth series (i.e. The Lord of the Rings).

Apple TV+ ($4.99 / month)

Apple TV+ is a no brainer if you just bought an Apple TV; it comes with a year of the service for free. The lineup of TV shows and movies is a bit light, but there is a lot of original content in the works. Apple has said they are more concerned with quality over quantity, so you can expect some great shows from them in the future.

Disney+: ($6.99 / month)

If you have kids in the house, then this just makes sense; Disney has opened their vaults and nearly all the classics are here (not to mention Disney's other companies' catalogues: Star Wars, Pixar, Marvel, and even some of Universal's—including The Simpsons).

YouTube Premium (starting at $11.99 / month)

YouTube Premium lets you watch YouTube content without ads. It also has original content—the most popular is probably Cobra Kai (the Karate Kid series). There are family and student rates.

Paramount (starting at $5.99 / month)

If you are a Star Trek fan, then you'll love this service—that's where you'll find the newest Star Trek TV series; that's also where you'll find the Good Fight (the legal drama that spun off from the award winning TV show The Good Wife); finally, that's where you'll find the new version of The Twilight Zone. You'll also find episodes of CBS shows that just aired the day before (depending on where you live, you might also get a live feed); you'll also have access to older shows like Cheers and Twin Peaks.

Peacock (basic plans free; paid plans start at $4.99)

NBC got into the streaming wars this April. There are already originals (like a future Battlestar Galactica, and reboots of Punky Brewster and Saved by the Bell); they also have shows like The Office and Parks and Recreation.

HBO Max (starting at $14.99)

HBO is a little confusing. There was HBO; HBO Now; and now HBO Max! HBO Max is basically HBO with other things attached—like originals and DC comics shows and movies. It has HBO, obviously, but it also includes more content like The Big Bang Theory; there's also original content and movies; Wonder Woman even debuted here at the same time as the theatrical release. If you have AT&T as a wireless carrier, you may be able to get it free—they frequently run promos and bundles.

Showtime ($10.99 / month)
This is basically the same content that you get on the cable channel.

Starz: ($8.99 / month)
This is basically the same content that you get on the cable channel. Yes, I know I'm repeating myself, but there's nothing new to add here.

Cinemax ($9.99 / month)
This is basically the same content that you get on the cable channel. One thing to note here: you get it as a paid add-on through either Hulu or Amazon Prime video.

Epix ($5.99 / month)
This is basically the same content that you get on the cable channel.

ESPN+ ($4.99 / month)
The subscription sounds like you get all the sports you want, right? Not exactly. You get a lot of stuff here—like college sports, tennis, and more. But things like MBL and NHL are paid add-ons.

WWE Network ($9.99 / month)
If you love WWE wrestling, then this is the subscription for you.

Criterion Channel ($10.99 / monthly)
If you love Criterion movies, but don't want to buy

physical copies, then this is something you should consider.

BET+ ($9.99 / monthly)
Features new and original programing from BET; this is a pretty new streaming service and has an exclusive deal with Tyler Perry.

PBS Passport (starting at $5 / month)
Many PBS shows are on other streaming services; this is for the die-hard fans who believe in public broadcast and want to support it. Ask your accountant, because this is the one streaming service that might count as a charitable donation!

Acorn TV ($4.99 / month)
If you're tired of TV in the United States, then Acorn might be what you need. Acorn TV features TV shows from Canada, the UK, Australia and more.

Mubi ($10.99 / month)
If you like your movies on the artsy side, Mubi is a streaming service that offers curated movies that are more arthouse / indie than mainstream.

Sundance Now (starting at $6.99 / month)
The Sundance Film Festival is kind of like the Oscars for indie and arthouse films—many films screened here go on to be nominated for awards and are picked up by big studios. Sundance Now is

the streaming service of the company behind the festival. It offers the same kind of movies you might see screened at the festival. It also has original content.

Kanopy (free)

You certainly can't beat the price of Kanopy! It's free. Kind of! Kanopy is free if your public library or university subscribes. The way it works is a library (or university) will purchase a title (usually at a premium) and then can offer it to their patrons as a streaming service. So why kind of? Because not every library participates. So, while it is free, you have to find a library around you that offers it. Helpful tip: most libraries let you get a library card even if you don't live anywhere near the library; for example, I live in Orange County, but have a library card for Los Angeles County. It was free to get. I know a lot of libraries will even give you a free card if you live out of state. It never hurts to ask what their usage policy is. While you are at the library, ask what other apps they subscribe to; my library, for example, lets me remotely check out eBooks and audiobooks from my house; they go right onto my phone and I don't have to pay a dime (not even late fees since they automatically expire on the due date if I don't renew them).

Sony Crackle (free)

Crackle is great if you don't mind ads. It has both

hit movies (albeit usually older movies) and TV shows; the only catch is you have to watch ads.

History Vault ($4.99 / month)

The History Channel's streaming app offers thousands of documentaries and series that focus on history.

Hallmark Movies Now ($4.99 / month)

If you are a fan of tearjerker movies and romances, then you already know what Hallmark is! This is the steaming version of the popular channel.

BroadwayHD ($8.99 / month)

If you like Broadway, but don't live anywhere near New York, then you'll love this streaming service. It offers over 200 recordings of different plays.

B/R Live ($9.99 / month)

Soccer, lacrosse, and more are offered in this sports streaming app; the app also has event add-ons that you can pay for.

NFL Sunday Ticket (price varies—approx. $24 / month)

NFL Sunday Ticket is for people who want to watch that big NFL game.

NBA Team / League Pass (price varies)

The NBA lets you stream your favorite team or all teams. Pricing starts at $119.99 / year for one team and $199 / year for all teams.

NHL.TV (price varies)

The NFL lets you stream your favorite team or all teams. Pricing starts at $115.99 / year for one team and $144.99 / year for league games.

INDEX

W

ABOUT THE AUTHOR

Scott La Counte is a librarian and writer. His first book, Quiet, *Please: Dispatches from a Public Librarian* (Da Capo 2008) was the editor's choice for the Chicago Tribune and a Discovery title for the Los Angeles Times; in 2011, he published the YA book The N00b Warriors, which became a #1 Amazon bestseller; his most recent book is *#OrganicJesus: Finding Your Way to an Unprocessed, GMO-Free Christianity* (Kregel 2016).

He has written dozens of best-selling how-to guides on tech products.

You can connect with him at ScottDouglas.org.